Lacordaire The Lawyer

Presentation

*Given at the Opening
of the Conference of* Lawyers

by

Joseph Brunhes

23 December 1898

Translated by

George Christian, OP

2017

Lacordaire The Lawyer

Honorable President,

Gentlemen,

I would reproach myself today for having accepted the task that I have to complete had I the liberty of doing so, and if the insistence of those who imposed it on me had not been a certain sign of benevolence.

Moreover, I could not better accede to your confidence in me, cherished collaborators, than by praising one of those who, among so many illustrious men which Burgundy proudly claims, more greatly enriched their native country by the brightness of their fame. And Lacordaire debuted so brilliantly at the bar of Paris that he acquired there an enviable reputation at a time when he was still on probation. He abandoned the order of lawyers, when much later, having become a priest, and plunged by the ardor of his zeal into the hazards of disputation, he had to remember, for his personal benefit, lessons that he had learned while defending the interests of others. I thought, Gentlemen, that I would find in his arguments a worthy manner of drawing your attention.

The preacher of Notre-Dame seems to have received from posterity the tribute of praise which he deserved: his name is almost always associated with those of Saint Bernard and of Bossuet, with whom Lacordaire is no doubt comparable, but not superior.

The lawyer, on the contrary, was misunderstood. And yet, nature, which had showed itself generous toward Lacordaire, had especially enriched him with the complex qualities that the profession of lawyer requires:

it seems to have predestined him for the bar. It would be easy to show that Lacordaire always allowed himself to be carried by the flow of that initial calling, that without realizing it, he remained faithful to it in the exercise of his religious ministry, that it was still as a lawyer that he preached, wearing the black robe of priest or the white robe of the Dominican.

But the already long story of his victorious arguments suffices to teach that today he would be counted among the masters of judicial eloquence if he had not stepped aside from the successes of the career that his talent insured.

"What the public especially likes in a lawyer, it is said[1], is his disinterest, his inborn hatred of injustice, his unshakable attitude in the defense of interests entrusted to him, the boldness of his language before the most powerful adversaries." An apt formula reveals the secret of the prodigious ascent that Lacordaire exercised on the crowds that flocked to listen to him, and sometimes even on those who judged him. He never ceded to anyone to satisfy indifference, he who gave up even the most human pleasures to fulfill the holy duties of the apostolate to which he felt himself called. More than anyone else, he was animated by an unshakable attitude in the defense of the interests entrusted to him, he who in open court did not fear to claim the rights of the Church in all their theological vigor, even with appropriate intransigence. Finally, no one before most powerful adversaries displayed a baffling boldness in their presence, no one as much as the young priest who was not intimidated by the solemn workings of the High Court, but who drew from his marvelous faculty of improvisation such eloquent words that many peers of France, oblivious of the thankless mission with which they had been burdened, let themselves fall into indulgent emotion.

*
* *

Jean-Baptiste-Henri Lacordaire was born at Recey-sur-Ource on 12 May 1802. His father, Nicolas Lacordaire, practiced as a medical doctor. His mother was the daughter of a lawyer in the parliament of Dijon. When she lost her husband prematurely, she remained a widow with four very young children, and sought consolation for her sorrow only in a rigorous fulfillment of her duties as a teacher. Solicitous of joining to her maternal tenderness the authority of an absent father, she gave her children unwavering affection. In 1812, Henri, the second child, entered the imperial college at Dijon. It was at this period of his life that faith eclipsed in his soul. "Soon," as he said, "the clouds thickened around me. A frosty night enveloped me on all sides, and I no longer received any sign of God's life in my soul."[2]

During his early scholastic years, he worked with only modest indolence; but before long, his natural abilities flowered. At the end of his studies, they won him first place. In rhetoric [second year of college], he earned the most desirable success: prizes of honor that the yearbook of the college perpetuated in recalling.

In addition, when he enrolled in law school, in 1819, his reputation as a formidable opponent had preceded him.

In the new sciences, whose examination he had undertaken and where he was to affirm his intellectual superiority, he had as professors men of high value: Proudhon, among others, is worthy of being cited. I would admit that Lacordaire, all the while praising their vigorous mind, felt that, as to the clarity of their exposition, his masters were too exclusively tied "to a technical teaching of articles of law mathematically joined together, without a look to the past, without an introduction to the eternal depths of the law, without reference to the general laws of human society, to a teaching, finally, unable to produce professionals to become great administrators, illustrious judges or genuine citizens[3]."

I would not have reported this reproach, assuredly unmerited, had it not been an interesting manifestation of Lacordaire in that it already revealed an intellect with powerful wings, always ready to take flight, in order to reach free summits, where the horizon has no limits.

On the school benches, the young student found Ladey again, whose friend he had been in college; he learned to be versed with Foisset, Boissard, Lorain, all of whom left lively remembrances in Burgundy. His heart opened gently to the entreaties of friendship; he enjoyed discrete pleasures, consoling intimacies, from which no whimsical awareness arose to trouble his serenity. In him, friendship was all powerful: it took over his heart and, purified it while absorbing in it all the sentimental feelings of his exuberant youth.

The union of Lacordaire with his friends did not have its source in a similarity of vulgar tastes, but in a common need for an ideal that, for them, who remained faithful to the faith of their childhood, found in him his natural and full satisfaction in the exercise of their Christian activity. At the time an unbeliever, he found this a painful expression in vague and restless aspirations. The activity proceeded, in his words, " from that mysterious sympathy which links vice to vice, mediocrity to mediocrity, but that also brings forth to the same hearth souls coming from higher up and seeking a better goal."⁴

This goal which at the time he expressed in obscure terms that later would be clarified for him in a supernatural light, was God – God whom unconsciously he had already been seeking because he had heretofore found Him.

The hour was favorable for the flourishing of the young minds. Châteaubriand placed at the service of the press the abundance of his talent; Lamartine prepared his first Meditations; Victor Hugo his first Odes; in Berryer, one could already detect one of the masters of the rostrum. This was the spring of the century; everywhere new life was spreading.

The youth of Dijon were dragged into this major movement of ideas. Lacordaire and his group founded an association that received the name "Society of Studies." It comprised four sections: philosophy, history, public law, literature. Lacordaire had himself inscribed in all four sections, and at the admission of his friends, held first place in each one of them. He pronounced defense arguments, so much had he received from nature the temperament of a lawyer. "He spoke," said Foisset, "as if to free himself from an internal demon agitating within him. Consequently there arose a plethora of arguments, an excitement of soul, something unexpected, and the good fortune of incomparable expressions."[5]

*
* *

In 1822, Lacordaire was certified in law. He left for the capital, carrying some modest savings painfully collected by his mother, and on 20 November, he took the oath of lawyer before the Royal Court of Paris. Upon the recommendations of Mr. Riambourg, president of the chamber at the Royal Court of Dijon, he presented himself to Mr. Alexandre Guillemin, at the time a lawyer at the Court of Appeals of Paris, and became his secretary. Concerning their relationship, Guillemin himself left us a touching statement:

"At the moment of his appearance at the bar of Paris, I became for the young Lacordaire," said he, "what is commonly called a patron, a kind of father, or perhaps an older brother."[6] He relates the conversation by which the modest probationer became his collaborator, then he adds: "For about eighteen months, Lacordaire gave evidence of all that could have been said about his remarkable intelligence, his lively imagination, as well as the candor of his character and his behavior. The reports and the consultations he composed, of which I have preserved a few manuscripts, always bore the imprint of his remarkable talent."

For his part, the young secretary was pleased to confide to his friends in Dijon all that he owed to the kindness of Mr. Guillemin. To work with such a master who under the cover of an apparent collaboration hides the lessons of a long experience, who defends the one associated in his work against a proud confidence in himself, but whom he also forewarns against useless discouragements, this is a privilege whose cost many of us know well. No one was more worthy of all this than Lacordaire.

In his early arguments, Lacordaire gave the measure of his talent. After hearing him, Berryer predicted for him a very glorious future. As for President Séguier, tradition holds that he expressed his admiration for Lacordairein these words: "Gentlemen, he is not Patru, he is Bossuet." "Lacordaire was not yet 22 years old, said Mr. Guillemin. Yet, notwithstanding the Ordinance of 20

November 1824 that was still observed at the time, Lacordaire pleaded without the magistrates inquiring about his age. His talent was the passport for his words."

Already a numerous clientele approached Lacordaire. " I now have three cases in my hands," he wrote to Ladey on 11 December 1822, "[7] one will be argued by me in a solemn audience. This is a magnificent legal case. It is a question of a natural child of the sister-in-law of the Prince of Wagram. Another, against four lawyers whom I accuse of forged writings in public documents. A third deals with a loan-shark in Langres, presenting interesting questions of the law." The accusation of forgery against the four lawyers seemed particularly to arouse his professional zeal. He speaks of this case with the naive pride of a novice surgeon who has just completed a significant operation."

Before long, he had the opportunity of studying more important matters. Guillemin, having accepted the position of lawyer at the Court of Appeals, kept beside him his intelligent collaborator. "The eloquence of Lacordaire," he wrote, "was better adapted for high-level discussions than for simple questions of law."

In the volume in which he reports his remembrances[8], Guillemin reproduces one memo written in his secretary's own hand, which I more than willingly cite in that biographers of Lacordaire seem to have ignored or overlooked its existence.

It was a question of the difficulty that arose from the first article of the law of 25 germinal year XI, as here stated: All adoptions made by an authentic act since 18 January 1792 up until the publication of the dispositions of the Civil Code dealing with adoptions will be valid even though they were not accompanied with any condition imposed since then for adopting or for being adopted.

This disposition had as its purpose to ratify even those adoptions that were tainted by a basic impediment, especially the adoption of children from adulterous relationships. This was the issue.

The initial opening was very worthy because of the eloquent power of the famous school of oratory that recruited in his generation, and reached its full flowering in 1830. Lacordaire approached the discussion by rising above the narrow interpretation of the law, by expressing himself thus:

"There is no doubt about the intention of the legislator. Called to cast light on muddled legislation (that of adoption), that had not received its extension and for which premature execution had created links and rights that it could not rescind without damaging the principle of non-retroactivity of laws, Lacordaire wished to spread a veil on the past so as not to require from it what it would impose in the future. But since the principle of adoption had been decreed, it does not follow that its unlimited spread extended to the violation of the general rules of law and the maxims of public order. When the law allows a new option, without specifying the method of its exercise, it is restricted, by the nature of things, to the major principles that dominate all legislation. Thus, since January 1792 up to April 1803, adoption remained in no way dependent on special formalities. It was fully justified and not to be annulled for lack of appropriate forms that the parties could not have foreseen."

Lacordaire then called to mind that the children of adultery were unable to inherit, and going back to the principle of this incapacity, concluded that children of adultery could not any more be adopted. "What does it matter," said he, "that inheritance and adoption rest on different bases, belong to two different orders of distinct ideas and that excluding one does not require the exclusion of the other. The child of adultery is not unable to be adopted because he is unable to inherit, but he is unable to inherit and be adopted because of his origins. To assure him rights reserved for legitimate children, and to raise him up to the honors of legitimacy is to attack marriage in its most inviolable privileges and to wrest from it everything that commands the respect of men and the faith of nations. This is what the legislators of 1793 envisioned, and which compelled them, reluctantly, to break the chain of their principles. This was an homage to the nature of things that interplay in the independence of men."

The young lawyer also resembled the Court of Appeals whose struggles were more congenial to his style. It is true that these do not always assure the superiority that these rigorous arguments deserved. It is true that sometimes these reserved the victory to certain of their reasons that the mind does not know. For all that, if it is easy to support them in a half-hearted fashion, it is not so easy to explain them as well as did Lacordaire, a powerful and original orator.

He himself relates his success to his friends left in Burgundy. On 3 August 1823, he wrote to Lorain: "I am pleading in the Court of Assizes, and succeeded in saving my client of the presumption of deceitful writing." The *Journal of Debates* named me in its issue of 26 July."[9] This issue which I was curious to read, in fact named only three individuals: Theodore Schwob, Abraham Jowan and Samson Franc who appeared in the Court of Assizes under the weight of an accusation of forgery and of swindling – no less surprising for the boldness of the maneuvers used than by the beginnings of success they had gained." They had sold several boxes that, according to their false declarations, were said to contain rolls of velvet. The buyer was content to examine the merchandise superficially. He noted that each of the rolls contained only a half-measure of velvet sewn at the end of scraps of old upholstery. The receipt delivered by the vendors carried an imaginary signature; this circumstance was intended to mask the swindling. The magazine added: "The attempt to mask counterfeiting was fought skillfully by Messrs. Pinet, Lacordaire, and Theodore Perrin, defender of the accused. Franc was completely acquitted; Jowan and Schwob were condemned of simple swindling: the first to three years, the second to two years in prison."

Lacordaire saw the horizon expand again and become brighter before him. Mr. Mourre, Attorney General for the Court of Assizes, who particularly noticed him, invited him to come and work at his office.

Nonetheless, the pleased beginner disregarded his personal success; the favors that fortune deigned to grant him did not take into account his invincible melancholia. "My thought," he wrote, "is longer-standing than is believed... I am filled with everything without having learned anything... Some speak of the glory of being an author, of public functions. Indeed I do have similar passing fancies; but, frankly, I have compassion for glory, and I cannot imagine how one could go to so much trouble to pursue this ridiculous little fool."

To success there follows trouble. This was an announcement of the revolution that was about to occur in him. Lacordaire underwent this crisis through which so many young souls pass, a crisis that, like all illnesses, has its characteristic manifestations. The young man sought in his surroundings the secret of his incomprehensible suffering. In a vexation full of bitterness, he flattered himself for no longer desiring happiness; and in his very words, "he asked everything vague and uncertain for an impression that would engage him while irritating him:" hours of sentimental restlessness, poorly-defined aspirations wherein even the most unreasonable of them battle in his mind with its very wrong mistrust of himself, wherein depended his irresolute decisions, like those of the pagan woman depicted by the writer Richepin:

Of the wind that will blow, of the manner in which the dawn will appear.[11]

After having suffered in all their fullness the sufferings of doubts, Lacordaire experienced with special intensity the joy that arises from certitude.

As soon as he had obtained such a strong possession of truth that he feared only the blunder that could undermine it, he approached his master. "On one of the early mornings of May 1824," wrote Guillemin, my "young collaborator entered my office and in emotional tone stated: I will be leaving you.– But why? We work so well together! – Furthermore, I am not moving to another section of law; but I have to reveal to you that I have been struggling for six months. Now, I believe, and with such conviction that there is no middle ground for me: I have to become a priest."

From the tone of his confidence, Guillemin understood that this conversion was not due to any whim of a mind lacking direction, nor to the abdication of a will submitting to authoritarian counselors. Besides, how could Lacordaire, the man of freedom, have admitted a belief imposed on him? "It was not," he wrote to his friend Boissard on 22 May

1824, "it was not that I endured a lengthy and imperceptible seduction from persons around me... I found the faith in my soul more as a remembrance than as a new gift."[12]

He himself identified precisely what in Catholicism had impressed and attracted him. It was in this way that quite rightly "when receiving religion as it is given, by professing it submissively in its entirety, some persons are attracted by certain truths, while other persons are attracted by certain other truths... For all that, they are no more nor less Christians. Basically, they are equally Christian, and in the same way, though not always for the same reasons. In the immense ocean of Christianity, this brings about variety, liberty under rule, and progress through unity.[13] Now in a phrase that we could believe flowed from the pen of some of our own contemporaries, Lacordaire made this significant admission: "I arrived at my Catholic beliefs through my social beliefs."[14]

*
*   *

It was on 12 May 1824, the twenty-second anniversary of his birth, that Lacordaire entered the seminary of Saint-Sulpice at Issy.

Withdrawn in this solitude, he seemed to have forever abandoned the struggles of the bar. "I am pleased at the future," he wrote to Ladey, "since I have placed it beyond the extent of this life. Besides, to live quietly and humbly is my sole ambition."[15]

He was strangely mistaken about his destiny, since he was to be involved in most passionate arguments and to appear before criminal jurisdiction.

Nonetheless, he initiated in a modest way his ecclesiastical functions: he was at first chaplain at a convent of Visitation Nuns. Before long, he received the duty of assistant to the chaplain of Henry IV College. In this role, he played a large part in the compilation of a report that the nine chaplains of colleges in Paris presented to the Minister of Public Instruction. In the circumstance of his position, among the petitioners, he played the role of lawyer-counselor. Later, he would present arguments in a process for which this report was both cause and pretext.

The signatories insisted on the difficulties they encountered in the exercise of their apostolate. Their grievances obtained singular authority in the existence of the University monopoly. When one institution is imposed by the State, its supporters are somewhat disarmed before those who would criticize them.

In his dream of Christianizing the young whose charge he had, would Lacordaire find encouragement and support from those who shared in his faith? Absolutely not. In fact, a wide political perception separated him from the greater number of them. The Catholic world of the day strongly relished a regime wherein religion received official honors. It went so far as to regret that the Bourbons were not autocratic. It did not notice that Catholicism would risk being compromised if religion were imposed by force along with a perishable dynasty – a tie-in that required the duty of fidelity. Lacordaire saw the danger. Following the constant teaching of the Church, he respected the form of the established government, but was fearful of the imprudent zeal some of his co-religionists professed for royalty. "I had remained," said he, "a liberal by becoming Catholic... Connecting the cause of Christianity to that of the Bourbons ran the same risks, and a priest who was not under this flag seemed to be an enigma to the more moderate and a kind of traitor to the most earnest."[16]

Unable to find in France employment appropriate to his activity, he dwelt on the thought of going to the United States, the country where liberty was developing like a natural product of the soil. But before embarking for the New World, he wanted to revisit the man whom he considered was at the time the founder of Christian and American liberty.[17] For a long time, Lamennais had made himself known.

Lacordaire had even approached him several times; until then, he simply had refused to follow him. "The philosophical system of *abbé* de La Mennais did not appear to him solid beyond all trials," said Spuller.[18] "His political opinions, his taste for monarchical traditions and his entire character displeased Lacordaire even more."

But since their fleeting meetings, an evolution had occurred in Lamennais's mind;

the two men would find themselves again on common ground.

Lamennais had recently suffered persecution because of cherished thoughts dear to his future disciple: ideas of independence regarding royalty and submission to the Pope, the supreme authority. Called before the tribunal of the Seine, and found guilty, he considered himself subsequently set fully free from all ties to the king and thereby ridding himself, by personal feelings, of this dynastic attachment, which was not shared by Lacordaire. He became busy with new conditions imposed on the future society by democracy and awaited from Christianity the necessary regeneration. Lacordaire had been troubled with the same thoughts. It was this community of worries and of hope that finally won over the suspicion that Lamennais had aroused in him.

In March 1830, Lacordaire took the road to Brittany, heading for *la Chenaie*. It was there in that out-of-the-way house in the woods that Lamennais assembled several disciples. His gentle and modest voice, as much as his sharp and proud pen, brought about a strange influence which Lacordaire could not escape. Together, they formulated grandiose plans and discontinued the project of going together to the New World in the coming spring. At least that is what Lacordaire wrote to Foisset on 19 July 1830.[19]

Ten days later, the Revolution erupted; Lamennais had foretold the fateful fall of royalty. The startling confirmation the events gave to his prediction only increased further his prestige.

The new era for which he had hoped was finally opening. The hour had come to bring about the vast program he had presented. The most efficacious way to proceed successfully was surely to use the power of the press. The journal *L'Avenir* was launched. As principal editors it had Lacordaire, Lamennais, *abbé* Gerbet, *abbé* Rohrbacher, de Coux, and vicount Charles de Montalembert. Within this group, you will see, Lacordaire filled a role that Lamennais would later define very exactly when he wrote to Montalembert: "Lacordaire fulfills among us the role of lawyer."[20]

On 20 August 1830 the prospectus of *L'Avenir* appeared. The journal was not slow in attracting the attention of the public and in arousing among numerous readers abundant admiration. More than 400,000 francs in subscriptions, obtained in only a few months, attest sufficiently to the ardent sympathies of its courageous editors, concerned before anything else, as Spuller said: "about the material and moral sufferings of the people, of [Christianity's] precarious place in society, of its right to claim a just share in the benefits of that civilization." [21]

Encouraged by these beginnings, the young writers believed themselves shielded against all lack of success. A page from the bulletin *Le Lycée*, strongly objected to the chaplains of colleges for their letter addressed to the ministers of public instruction in which they complained about the difficulties of their duties. Lacordaire who – you may remember – had largely collaborated in that missive, cited the journal for defamation before the criminal court. But in the course of the process, the Lawyer of the King argued that with the chaplains as public servants, only a jury could recognize the complaint. Lacordaire, throwing him several eloquent responses, was applauded by the audience. On leaving, one of the assistant clerks came to him, grasped his hand with emotion: "Reverend," said he, "you are a courageous man."[22]

And yet, the tribunal declared itself unqualified. The Attorney General, contrary to the conclusions arrived at in first instance by the agent of the public ministry, called for an appeal to this decision. He maintained before the Court that the priest could not be a public servant. Lacordaire then undertook to defend the same thesis. "What is a priest," he inquired. "A priest is a man who relates to other men the word of God and who blesses in His name... The priest is the speaker of that word, his function is to repeat it. From whom did he receive this duty? Only from Him who could give it: from God. Now God does not set up public servants; He sets up men... I know full well that there were times when the faith of men was disapproved of according to law, when liberty of conscience did not exist in the world. But those times are over. After several centuries of struggle, the blood of persons and the Charter of France were founded on religious liberty, which is imperishable. God became free with the liberty of the citizen. We claim nothing else for Him; we simply desire that He be a citizen of France.

At these words, the audience muttered. But Lacordaire quickly imposed silence on it, while addressing to them these words: "Gentlemen, I can think of no better designation than to be called a citizen of France, a better way to be free than to carry the name. I would gladly give it to Him who dared to become the slave of men so as to acquire their freedom."[23]

Lacordaire then undertook the same thesis. "What is a priest," he inquired. A priest is a man who related to other men the word of God and who blesses in his name. The priest is the speaker of that word. From whom did he receive this duty? Only from him who could give it: from God. Now God does not set up public servants; He sets up men. I know full well that there were times when the faith of men was disapproved of according to law, when liberty of conscience did not exist in the world. But those times are over. After several centuries of struggle, the blood of persons and the Charter of France were founded on religious liberty, which is imperishable. God became free with the liberty of the citizen. We claim nothing else for Him, we simply desire that He be a citizen of France.

Then he took up, without confusion, the interrupted discussion. But his conclusions and those of the Attorney General were definitively rejected. A few months later, the Supreme Court condemned the system of the Court of Paris by rejecting a similar warrant in an identical case.

Lacordaire quickly forgot that failure to get involved in a more passionate process. He had played the role of plaintiff, now he was going to play that of accused.

*
* *

In *L'Avenir*'s edition of 25 November 1830, Lacordaire had addressed to the bishops of France a frankly cruel article that the right of nominating bishops by the king had been, in his eyes, an abuse.

The following day's issue contained an article by Lamennais, no less violent, which bore the title: "Oppression of Catholics." The Government was just waiting for an occasion to strike *L'Avenir*. It hurriedly presented to the Court of Assizes a two-fold charge of disobedience to the law and incitation of hatred and disrespect to the government of the King, citing the two authors along with M. Waille, general editor of the paper.

The case was judged on 30 January 1831, under the presidency of Mr. Taillandier. A great crowd filled the precincts of the Court of Assizes. Already the politics excited interest especially among the female public, if we believe the *Journal des Débats* [Record of Cases]. Women had flocked in great numbers to this session. The indictment had been entrusted to Mr. Berville, Attorney General. A refined individual with perfect tact, he executed this delicate task with capable moderation. He expressed his regret in having to pursue these men whose cause was, basically, his own. He limited himself to reproaching the accused for the intemperance of their language, their emotional arguments.

Mr. Janvier, of the Angers bar, whom Lamennais had chosen as defender, then spoke. In language in which the correction aligned itself with the eloquence, he attempted to justify the ultramontane theories of his illustrious client. He finished speaking at a late hour. The session was interrupted, but resumed at eight o'clock at night for the presentation by Lacordaire in his personal case and that of Lawyer Charles Ledru for Mr. Waille.

It was in the solemnity of a hearing in the evening that *abbé* Lacordaire appeared at the bar, dressed in the gown of a lawyer.

"Gentlemen," said he, "I was still very young when I first saw this capital wherein curiosity, imagination, the thirst for knowledge, led me to believe that the secrets of the world would be revealed to me. The weight overpowered me, and here I was a Christian, I was a priest! Allow me to rejoice in it, Sirs, because I never knew freedom as much as on the day when with the holy anointing, I received the right to speak in God's name. The world opened up before me, and I realized that there was in man something inalienable, something of the divine: the spoken word."

"I protested against the nomination of bishops by civil power; I am mistaken, emanating from our oppressors, this is the term that I used, and as the Attorney General long stopped using it, I will do the same. Our oppressors! This word has disturbed you; you ask me to explain. You have only to look at my hands to see that they had been only two things bruised by shackles. My hands are free, Mr. Attorney General, but my hands are not all of me. Me! What is me is my thought, it is my speech. And so you well know, I find my word oppressed in my country, this divine in me, this thought, this word, in sum: me, as a person."

Yes, you do not bind my hands; how little this would bother me because it would be justice or violence. Justice would not be oppression, nor would violence. There would remain against oppression only violence! But if you do not bind my hands, you bind my thought: you do not allow me to teach, me, to whom it was said: *teach*. The seal of your laws is on my lips; when will it be broken? I have, therefore, called you my oppressors, and I am apprehensive about the bishops who came from your hands...."

"I was aware, Sirs, of those injuries to my brothers. I raised for them and for myself a voice animated by feelings of our dignity, common to everyone, because we, and those with us, we are citizens of France, of that free country to which everyone is accountable for his honor, held to defend her, held to push aside injury and oppression. This I have done, insofar as it depended on me."

"My work is accomplished. Yours, Gentlemen, is to release me, fully absolved of this accusation. It is not simply for myself that I request this. There are two things that bestow genius: God and a jail cell. Therefore, I should not fear one more than the other. But I call for my acquittal by taking a step toward the union of faith and freedom, as a pledge of peace and reconciliation. And there you have it, Sirs; I propose that you acquit Jean-Baptiste-Henri Lacordaire, in the understanding that he never fell, that he conducted himself as an honest citizen, that he defended his God and his freedom. And I will do this all my life, Sirs."[25]

The priest who claimed his right to liberty so eloquently had not yet reached the age of thirty.

Moved by such generous courage, the jury acquitted both him and his co-accused. When at midnight the resolution was proclaimed, the audience exploded in applause.

And yet, this human glory did not silence in Lacordaire the virtues of the apostle. "After the crowd had left," wrote Montalembert, "we returned alone, Lacordaire and I, in the dark along the quays. He was neither overwhelmed nor elated by his triumph. I noticed that for him these minuscule vanities of success were less than nothing, dust in the night."[26]

Public opinion echoed with manifestations of warm sympathy for the accused.

Even *le Globe*, that already had inspired the followers of Saint-Simon and who certainly had not always treated Lamennais and his disciples with respect, wrote on 2 February 1831: "*L'Avenir* has been vindicated; it is an homage that the jury gave to religious liberty. They realized that it was not theirs to make themselves arbiters of the faith. The Catholic religion had previously rendered such great service to humanity as to gain today the right to tolerance, especially when it is personified in men of courage and of talent."

The growing influence of the young school awoke fears in government circles. The bar itself was unable to defend itself against a certain uneasiness.

On 24 November, Lacordaire had written to the President of the bar the following letter.

"Sir, it was eight years ago that I began my probation at the bar of Paris. I interrupted it at the end of eighteen months to devote myself to religious studies, which later allowed me to enter into the Catholic hierarchy; today I am a priest. Now that major events have changed the position of the Church in the world, she needs to break all the ties that bound it to the State and to bring about new ones with the people. This is why, devoted more than ever to her service, to her laws, to her worship, I find it useful to get closer to my fellow citizens while pursuing my career at the bar. I have the honor of alerting you, Sir, even though I can foresee no obstacle of my part from the rules of the Order" [regulations of the legal establishment].

The Counsel, hesitating, deferred its answer.

In the meantime, Lacordaire appeared before the Court of Appeals. As soon as the Order of lawyers learned the verdict of acquittal, it resolved to choose a side. Lacordaire would certainly be a compromising member. The situation was opportune to cool his indiscreet zeal. The Council rejected his request. This decision was generally disapproved by the press. The *Gazette des Tribunaux* [The magazine of court activities], among others, criticized it strongly. Did the Council of Order pretended to safeguard the dignity of the priest and to defend Lacordaire from his own imprudence? Its role as protector rarely was part of its duties. Only the hierarchical superiors of Lacordaire were authorized to address to him their well-advised rebukes.

The young *abbé* did not long remain a lawyer *in partibus*. Circumstances soon presented him with a solemn occasion to reappear at the bar.

*
* *

In its final article, the Charter of 1830 declared that it would allow in the briefest time possible public instruction and freedom of teaching. But the authorities did not seem disposed to honor their decision. Much more, so as to deny the partisans their last hopes for freedom, the University had just deprived the priests of Lyons of the right to teach their choirboys, at no cost to them, lessons in Latin. Lacordaire commented on this fact with indignation in *L'Avenir* of 3 April 1831. The entire press, the editors of the *Globe*, were both the first to call for the emancipation of teaching. But the eloquent protests did not satisfy Lacordaire's ardent conviction. He decided to open a school with cost-free instruction, without waiting for the law that was to regulate the application of the principle of freedom contained in the Charter. Lamennais remained outside this attempt. Only Montalembert and de Coux added their bold activity to that of Lacordaire. The prospect of a pitiless repression in no way frightened them. They had announced in *L'Avenir* the date of the opening, and even alerted, in proper fashion, the prefect of police.

On 9 May, after some words by Lacordaire, classes began. But the zeal of the young professors was not exercised for very long. On the next day, 10 May, an official came to enjoin them to close the school. In vain did they protest; the intervention of several police constables of the city forced them to submit.

The public minister hastened to cite them before the Court of Petty Sessions, but he had not taken into account an adversary whom serious studies and the practice of the law had made familiar with rules more subtle than our laws, and who knew very well all the resources that the Code of Criminal Instruction offered to a knowledgeable interpreter. Very capably, Lacordaire pleaded the incompetence of the tribunal. He argued that in any case, the court could only find him guilty of a political fault, that the knowledge of matters belonged only to a jury. Foisset reported the impressions of someone in attendance. "One had to hear his voice, to see his taut neck, his lips pale and quivering, his overwhelming gestures. Strong and passionate applause interrupted him at various moments. One could easily imagine the effect that he produced when, invoking like St.

Paul, the right of a citizen, he pronounced these word of the Apostle: *Caesarem appello,* which he translated boldly as *I appeal to the Charter."*

In its conclusions, the tribunal rightly declared itself incompetent. Here are found several incidents of procedure that biographers of Lacordaire did not mention. The king's lawyer objected to the decision of the tribunal. The matter was remanded to the Court; since the accused did not appear, the Court condemned them *in absentia*. The latter quickly objected to the arrest, and the matter was again presented at the next level when Count Montalembert died, leaving his son to inherit the rank of peer. The young Charles de Montalembert claimed the right to be judged by the Court of Peers, and Lacordaire with de Coux claimed the same privilege, invoking very legally the principle of the indivisibility of the proceedings.

It was on Monday, 19 September 1831, that the three accused appeared before the Peers of France. The charge was upheld in a vulgar manner by Mr. Persil, Attorney General. In order to show his good nature toward power, he exaggerated excessively the wrongs of the accused. He went so far as to reproach them "for having attempted to corrupt youth by an illegal action, and inviting them to find knowledge in an establishment whose first principle was revolution and disobedience to existing laws."[28]

Frémery and Lafargue, lawyers for the defense, then spoke. Using the Charter as their basis, they attempted to establish that freedom of instruction has existed irrevocably on the day when the king and the nation had authorized it. It did not matter that a later act had not organized that freedom: it existed, that was enough.

Then the accused stood up on their own behalf. At first, it was Montalembert. He abandoned the legal grounds to place himself on Catholic grounds. His young age, his status as orphan, touched everyone.

De Coux followed him; but, profoundly moved, he had trouble completing his presentation.

The Attorney General then answered the lawyers. His role was an easy one: he followed an orator who had not produced a favorable impression on the Court. The defense appeared compromised when Lacordaire stood up. He had reserved for himself the most dangerous task, that of giving the final words in favor of the accused. Based on the genius of his ability at extemporary speaking, he directed this reply that remained famous.

"Noble Peers,"

52

"I look around and I am stunned. I am stunned to see myself in the docket of the accused, while the Attorney General occupies the seat of the Public Minister. I am stunned that the Attorney General dared to stand as my accuser, he who is capable of the same offense as me, and who committed it in the very precincts where he accused me, before all of you, not so long ago. Indeed, what does he accuse me of? To have used the right written in the Charter and not regulated by a law. Previously, he had asked of you the heads of four ministers, in virtue of a right written in the Charter, one not regulated by a law! If he was able to do this, then I also could do it, with the difference being that he asked for blood, and I simply wanted to offer free instruction to children of the people. Both of us, acted in the name of article 69 of the Charter. If Mr. Attorney General is guilty, how can he accuse me? If he is innocent, how can be continue to accuse me?"

"I have other reasons to be stunned, noble Peers; since the guard of honor at your doors has violated, as I did, in the same meaning, the existing laws. Long before the national army received the organization promised to it by the Charter, and when it was still under the blow of the ordinance that had destroyed it, it was shaped, it elected chiefs, it appeared under arms, not in one section of France, but over the entire extent of the country. How is it that wherever my eyes fall, they find accomplices and yet both I and my friends are the only ones on the bench of the accused? One could ask for the head of the ministers in virtue of the principle of freedom not organized by a law. And when we wanted, in virtue of a principle of freedom not organized by a law but written on the same page and in the same article of the Charter, to assemble a few children of poor families to teach them the elements of divine and human knowledge, some came against us as if we were disturbers of public peace; our children were chased out, my residence was taken from me; my door is still under seal. I have seen nothing in the Attorney General's speech that explains such impunity on the one hand and so much strictness on the other, unless impunity be justice and rigor be persecution. Now I understand both of them, and after persecution, noble Peers, I dare to claim justice..."

"If I had the time, I would have granted the public ministry all that it desired, And, supposing that we were guilty of the violation of a decree entailing a penalty, I would have taken from my guilt the same proof of innocence. Indeed, noble Peers, there are godly faults, and the violation of a law can sometimes be the accomplishment of a higher law. In the first case of freedom of instruction, in the famous case in which Socrates lost his life, he was clearly guilty of offending the gods and consequently against the laws of the country.

And yet, the posterity of pagan nations and the posterity of the centuries since Christ branded his judges and his accusers. They absolved only the guilty and the executioner; the guilty because he broke the laws of Athens in order to obey more important laws; the executioner, because he handed over the cup while sobbing. And I, noble Peers, I would have proved to you that while trampling on this decree of the Empire, I had certainly upheld the laws of my country, served well its freedom – and served the cause and the future of all Christian peoples. But time has robbed me of my thoughts; yet I forgive it, since it leaves me your justice. And that is sufficient. When Socrates in that first and famous cause of freedom of instruction, was about to leave his judges, he exclaimed: 'We will leave; you to live, I to die.' This is not, my noble judges, the way we leave you. Whatever your judgment, we will leave to live because freedom and religion are immortal, and the feelings of a spotless heart, that you have heard from our mouth will not, for all that, perish."²⁹

At those closing words, the gallery burst into applause.

The Court deliberated a long time. Many of the judges, overcome by emotion, spoke in favor of the accused. But certain partisans of authoritarian tradition were indignant at the scandal of the defense and finally obtained the condemnation of each of the accused to paying 100 francs.

*
* *

The series of judicial troubles was over. *L'Avenir* would suffer other obstacles but I could not dwell on them without leaving my subject. Nonetheless, they move me to a reflection that I would like to offer you. It seems to me that under the circumstances, Lacordaire no doubt conducted himself as a Christian, but also as a man to whom the attributes and the exercise of the profession of lawyer have given the habit of agreeing in advance to the decisions of authorities which he recognizes as necessary and legitimate.

One is aware of the protests that arose from a great number of Catholics concerning the teachings of *l'Avenir*, Lacordaire, Montalembert, and Lamennais, based on their good faith, which those protestors carried the argument before the Court of Rome.

The effort was imprudent; on certain ideas of *l'Avenir*, Rome could maintain a benevolent silence but could not give positive approbation.

It is appropriate, however, to forestall a confusion that is often expressed in speaking of the liberalism of Lacordaire. His teaching was not that of the liberal parties of rhe Restoration and of the Monarchy of July, inheritors of Gallican traditions for whom the seizure by civil power over the Church seemed to guarantee essentially the freedom of the State. No one more than Lacordaire attacked these pretensions nor was it the Pope who blamed them.

Neither was Lacordaire's liberalism mixed in with economic teachings that exaggerated all legislative intervention regarding labor to the point of rejecting all legislative intervention between owners and workers. We should not forget that it was to Lacordaire that we owe this statement: "In the struggle between the strong and the weak, it is the law that frees and freedom that oppresses." We cannot deny that again on this point, the Church could offer him effective justification.

But at the time, Lacordaire was

struggling; the questions of politics and of society were not clearly separated, freedom and liberalism seemed to be synonymous terms. The principles of 1789 owed their prestige to being attacked as targets by an appropriately unpopular group, and perhaps more because they had not yet explored all their economic consequences. We can easily understand that the most fruitful beliefs were not thrown into the mix except when allied to certain teachings to which the Church could not give the seal of orthodoxy.

This explains the condemnation of *l'Avenir* in 1812.

Lacordaire bowed down before the decision of the Pope, as a lawyer, respectful of the decisions of justice.

By the loyalty of his obedience, he created for himself one more claim to the confidence of ecclesiastical authorities, while Lamennais boxed himself in a hostility that would shortly lead him to a complete rupture with the Church.

After three years of peaceful contemplation, Lacordaire again took the pulpit at Notre-Dame.

There, once more, I could have shown you that he employed all the qualities of the bar. Suffice for me to say that in the Cathedral of Paris, he spoke much less as a rigorous theologian than as an ardent defender of the cause of the Church – that he was in fact the advocate for God before the jury that filled the immense nave.

You understand, Gentlemen, that Lacordaire was the quintessential lawyer. To sum up in a few words, he reconciled in himself those contrary qualities that honor the Bar:

independence and submission: independence of his convictions, and submission to the authority charged with keeping it in check; – pride and modesty: proud for his ideas, and modesty as regards himself.

We would not have to look for models in past history if this were a single example of men, who, by the turmoil of events were thrown into public life in spite of themselves, men who bequeathed to posterity the remembrance of their struggles and revealed to it the secret of their power.

ENDNOTES

1. Maurice Joly: *Le Barreau de Paris*, p. XXII.

2. *Le Testament du P. Lacordaire*, publié par le comte de Montalembert, p. 15.
   [The Testament of Lacordaire in English exists, see: www.worksofLacordaire.com]

3. *Le Testament du P. Lacordaire*, p. 38.

4. *Le Testament du P. Lacordaire*, p. 38.

5. Foisset, *Vie du R. P. Lacordaire*, p. 42 [Available in English through Amazon]

6. Alexandre Guillemin, *Le Souvenir du ciel dans les émotions de la terre*, p. 247.

7. Lacordaire, Lettres nouvelles publiées par Mme Victor Ladry et M. P. de Viré, - Delhomme

et Briguet, 1895, p. 9.

8. *Le Souvenir du ciel dans les émotions de la terre.*

9. H. Lacordaire, *Lettres nouvelles*, p. 48.

10. Lettre citée par le P. Chocarne, *Vie du P. Lacordaire*, p. 44.

11. *Les Martyrs,* Acte I, Scène III.

12. H. Lacordaire, Lettres nouvelles, p. 95.

13. P. Brunetière. Conférence sur "l'éloquence de Bossuet" faite à Dijon le 15 avril 1894, réproduite dans le journal *Le Temps* du 25 avril 1891.

14. Lettre à Lorain, 15 mars 1821, citée par Foisset, Vie du R. P. Lacordaire, p. 59.

15. Lettre à Ladey, 9 juillet 1824. H. Lacordaire, *Lettres nouvelles*, p. 102.

16. Testament du P. Lacordaire, p. 47.

17. Lettre à Lorain, citée par Foisset, *Vie du R. P. Lacordaire*, p. 42.

18. E. Spuller, *Lamennais*, p. 168.

19. Foisset, Vie du R. P. Lacordaire, p. 47.

21. E. Spuller. Lamennais, p. 175.

22. Détail rapporté par M. d'Haussonville, auteur de l'ouvrage consacré à Lacordaire, dans la collection des grands écrivains français publié par la librairie Hachette.

23. L'Avenir, n° 97.

24. Numéro du 1er février 1831.

25. *L'Avenir* du 8 février 1831, n° 115.

26. *Le P. Lacordaire*, par de Montalembert, p. 34.

27. Foisset, *Vie du R. P. Lacordaire*, p. 171.

28. *L'Avenir*, supplément du 21 septembre 1831, n° 340.

29. *L'Avenir*, n° 341.

For a fuller account of the issue, see *L'Avenir Law Suit* in: www.worksoflacordaire.com, also translated by George Christian , OP.

www.ingramcontent.com/pod-product-compliance
Lightning Source LLC
Chambersburg PA
CBHW021025180526
45163CB00005B/2122